Nuclear Waste

Kate Scarborough

Bridgestone Books

an imprint of Capstone Press
Mankato, Minnesota

Originally published as Nuclear Waste, ©2002 Franklin Watts, United Kingdom

Bridgestone Books are published by Capstone Press
151 Good Counsel Drive, P.O. Box 669, Mankato, MN 56002
http://www.capstone-press.com

Library of Congress Cataloging-in-Publication Data

Scarborough, Kate.
   Nuclear waste / by Kate Scarborough.
      v. cm. -- (Our planet in peril)
Includes bibliographical references and index.
Contents: What is nuclear waste? -- The world's energy needs -- Fossil
fuels -- Nuclear energy -- Background radiation -- Nuclear power
stations -- Nuclear waste -- Low level and intermediate waste -- High
level waste -- Further research -- Nuclear fusion -- Public concerns --
The future of nuclear power.
   ISBN 0-7368-1362-4 (hardcover)
   1. Radioactive wastes--Juvenile literature. 2. Nuclear
energy--Juvenile literature. [1. Radioactive wastes. 2. Nuclear
energy.] I. Title. II. Series.
   TD898 .S39 2003
   363.72'89--dc21

                                              2002010139

Editor: Kate Banham   Illustrations: Ian Thompson
Designer: Kelly-Anne Levey   Picture Research: Diana Morris
Art Direction: Jonathan Hair   Consultant: Sally Morgan, Ecoscene

Acknowledgements

The publishers would like to thank the following for permission to reproduce
photographs in this book.

Toshiyuki Aizawa/Reuters/Popperfoto: 28-29b; Klaus Andrews/Still Pictures: 5t, 20b;
Martin Bond/Environmental Images: 16tr, 17b; William Campbell/Still Pictures: 16tl, 17t;
Philip Carr/Environmental Images: 29t; Fred Dott/Still Pictures: 8tr; David Drain/Still
Pictures: 4bl; Mark Edwards/Still Pictures: 18-19t; Index/Stock/Harry Walker: 8b; Vasily
Fedoseev/Reuters/Popperfoto: 16b; Dylan Garcia/Still Pictures: 23b; Herbert
Giradet/Environmental Images: 9t; Pierre Gleizes/Environmental Images: 12b, 18b;
Pierre Gleizes/Still Pictures: 19t, 26b; Angela Hampton/ Ecoscene: 6t; Paul
Harrison/Still Pictures: 12-13t; Nick Hawkes/Ecoscene: 15b; Hibbert/Ecoscene: 13b;
Reinhard Janke/Still Pictures: 15t; Layne Kennedy/ Corbis: 27t; Graham
Kitching/Ecoscene: 4tr; Noel Matoff/Still Pictures: 26t; Juan Carlos Munoz/Still
Pictures: 25c; Jean-Francois Mutzig/Still Pictures: 21t; NASA/Still Pictures: 24t; Shehzad
Noorani/Still Pictures: 6b; Trevor Perry/ Environmental Images: 5b; Thomas
Raupach/Still Pictures: 19b, 29c; Roger Ressmeyer/Corbis: 25b; Department of Energy
(DOE): 27b; Harmut Schwarzbach/Still Pictures: 14c, 28-29t; Paul Seheult/Eye
Ubiquitous: 13tr; Photo courtesy of U.S. Department of Energy: 21b; Sabine Vielmo/Still
Pictures: front cover; Adam Woolfit/Corbis: 22t; Dave Wootton/Ecoscene: 7b.

Contents

Words printed in *italics* are explained in the glossary.

What is nuclear power?

The nuclear power industry has developed over the last 50 years to create large amounts of electrical *energy* that can light cities. But nuclear power stations also produce waste. This waste causes concern for the *environment*.

A huge amount of energy is needed to light up a city like New York.

Sellafield nuclear power station in Cumbria, United Kingdom.

Why do we need nuclear power?

Electricity is *generated* mainly using coal and oil (also called *fossil fuels*), but demand for electricity is growing faster than these fuels can supply it. Nuclear power can generate enormous amounts of energy without using fossil fuels. Countries such as France and Japan do not have natural sources of fossil fuels. Instead of buying oil and coal, they prefer to rely on nuclear power.

Because nuclear waste is so dangerous, people have to wear special protective suits when working with it. The suits must cover them completely.

What is wrong with nuclear power?

The major problem with nuclear power is its waste. The material left over after electricity has been produced is extremely dangerous to all life. It is *radioactive* and severely damages living *cells* that are exposed to it. Plants wither and die. Animals and people can develop cancers and die.

Dealing with nuclear waste

No one has yet found a way to make nuclear waste totally safe. So far, the waste is buried or covered heavily in concrete in hopes that its effects are controlled. Scientists continue to work on treating waste more effectively.

Burning fossil fuels releases clouds of potentially harmful gases into the atmosphere.

In 50 years

The United States and Europe use most of the electrical power in the world. However, China and India's demands for electricity are growing rapidly. Scientists think that in 50 years, the world's electrical needs will more than double. If fossil fuels create this electrical energy, *global warming* could have disastrous effects on world climate. If nuclear power is used, large quantities of highly harmful waste material will need to be stored.

The world's energy needs

A modern kitchen contains kettles, cookers, microwaves, refrigerators, and other appliances that run on electricity.

Different types of energy are used to create movement and warmth, power a radio, or light a room. As the world's population rises, more energy is needed to make sure that people can travel and live in comfort.

How much fuel do we use?

One way to see how much energy is used is to look at oil. In 1999, the world used more than 5 billion gallons (20 billion liters) of oil. Coal and natural gas are also used, as well as nuclear energy and other energy sources.

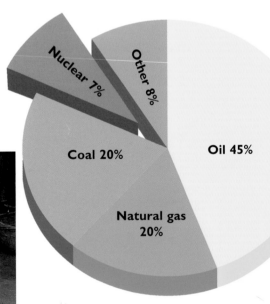

Nuclear 7%

Other 8%

Coal 20%

Oil 45%

Natural gas 20%

The percentages of fuels used in the world in 2000.

In many developing countries such as Bangladesh, food is cooked over a fire.

How much energy do you use?

If you have a dishwasher, oven, refrigerator, washing machine, stereo, TV, and toaster in your kitchen, you use the equivalent of about 115 gallons (435 liters) of oil a year to keep them working.

Dishwasher	Oven	Refrigerator	Washing Machine
24 gallons	22 gallons	34 gallons	26 gallons
91 liters	83 liters	128 liters	98 liters

TV	Toaster	Stereo
6 gallons	1 gallon	2 gallons
23 liters	4 liters	8 liters

The growing need for energy

In 1999, the United States, with a population of more than 284 million, used 25 percent of all the energy produced in the world. Compare this to countries with very large populations such as China (more than 1.3 billion), which used 8 percent, and India (more than 1 billion), which used 3 percent. Scientists *forecast* that over the next 20 years, the greatest expansion of fuel usage will be in the developing world, especially Asia and South America. Experts predict that by 2020, global energy use will rise by 59 percent. Most of this increase will be found in Asia.

On average, each person in the United States uses two times as much energy as someone in Europe and about 10 times as much as a person in China.

Crops today are harvested with machines that use large amounts of energy from fossil fuels.

Fossil fuels

Fossil fuels are found in the ground in the form of oil, coal, and gas. They have developed over millions of years. The usefulness of fossil fuels as energy sources was discovered in the 1800s. Using fossil fuels has two major drawbacks. Fossil fuels release gases that pollute the atmosphere, and their supply may run out.

Oil and coal

Oil and coal resources have formed over the last 350 million years from dead plant and animal life. The resources have been found all over the world. Today, oil and coal are used mainly for transportation—most cars, trains, and airplanes run on oil—and for generating electricity in power stations.

Oil rigs like this one retrieve oil from deep under the seabed.

Coal-fired power stations release gases that may harm our atmosphere.

Natural gas

Experts believe greater use of natural gas will reduce the amount of *carbon dioxide* emitted into the air compared to burning coal and oil. Many new power stations are gas-fired.

These trees have been damaged by acid rain resulting from burning fossil fuels.

Waste products

Burning oil and coal to release their energy also releases the gases carbon monoxide and carbon dioxide into the air. Scientists believe carbon dioxide causes climate change by acting with the Sun to warm the atmosphere. This warming is known as the *greenhouse effect*. Other elements released by burning fossil fuels include sulfur and nitrogen. These elements combine with the water vapor in the atmosphere to form acids that damage both animal and plant life. This is acid rain.

Are supplies running out?

It is not easy to calculate how much oil, coal, and natural gas are still available. Scientists generally think there will be enough coal for a few more centuries, but oil and gas will be in short supply within a few decades. All the fossil fuels that have developed over millions of years will be completely used up in just a few hundred years. Alternative energy sources, such as nuclear power, are needed.

◆ Science in action

Test the greenhouse effect.

You will need 2 glass bowls, a piece of glass, and 2 thermometers.

Place a thermometer in each bowl and place both bowls in the sun. Carefully place the piece of glass over one bowl. After an hour, check the temperature in both bowls. Which is hotter? The glass cover acts like the greenhouse gases in our atmosphere. It traps heat from the Sun, raising the air temperature in the bowl in the same way gases trap heat, raising the temperature of the environment.

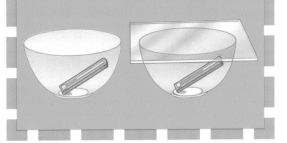

Nuclear energy

Nuclear energy gets its name from the *nucleus*, the central part of an *atom*. Everything in the world is made of different types of atoms. An element is something that is made of only one type of atom.

What is an atom?

Atoms consist of of three different *particles*: neutrons, protons, and electrons. The nucleus contains protons and neutrons. Electrons circle the nucleus. The number of each particle differs for every element. Hydrogen is the smallest atom with just one electron and one proton. *Uranium* is a large atom with 92 electrons, 92 protons, and 143 neutrons. Most elements are stable. Their atoms always keep the same balance of these particles. Some elements are unstable. Their atoms continually change by emitting some of these particles. Unstable elements are radioactive.

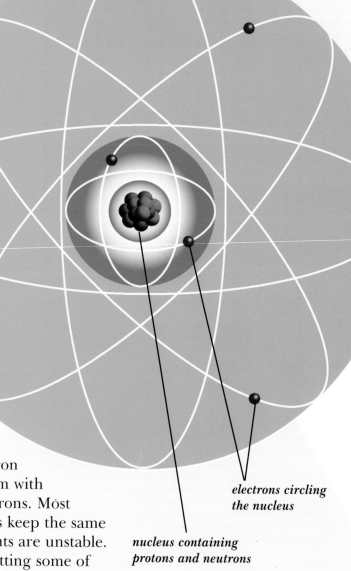

electrons circling
the nucleus

nucleus containing
protons and neutrons

Radioactive elements

When an atom changes, it releases energy. In radioactive elements, the energy is released in the form of heat, light, and *radiation*. Radiation can be particles or rays of matter.

Alpha particles

An alpha particle is a combination of neutrons and protons emitted by the nucleus. This radiation does not travel far and is stopped by most solid objects.

alpha particle

new atom formed

Beta particles

A beta particle is an electron sent out by the nucleus. This radiation travels a few yards and can go through human bodies but is stopped by metals.

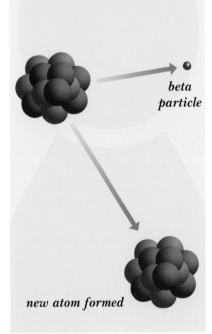

beta particle

new atom formed

Gamma rays

Sometimes the nucleus emits a wave of energy, called gamma radiation rays. These waves travel several miles but can be stopped by lead or thick concrete.

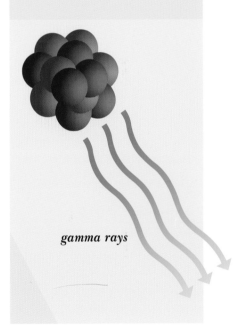

gamma rays

Neutrons

Sometimes the nucleus breaks down, emitting streams of neutrons. Neutrons travel even farther than gamma rays but can be stopped by anything containing hydrogen, such as water.

Half-life

To understand more about the use of radiation, it is important to know about half-life. Half-life is the time a radioactive element takes to lose half of its radiation. The next half of the radioactive decay can take thousands of years. For example, Carbon 14 is a radioactive atom with a half-life of 5,700 years. If you start with 100 atoms of Carbon 14, after 5,700 years, you would have about half of them left. After another 5,700 years, you would have 25 atoms left, and so on.

Background radiation

Radiation is the release of energy as waves or particles. It can take the form of light and sound, as well as radioactive rays. Radiation is a natural part of the universe. Every day, people come across radiation from many sources. This kind of radiation is known as "background radiation."

Granite rocks often contain radioactive material.

Radiation from the Sun

In the 1930s, Austrian scientist Victor Franz Hess discovered that the Sun and other stars continually bombard the Earth with radiation. Hess found radiation levels increased the farther people got from the Earth's surface. People traveling in an airplane are more affected by radiation than people on the ground.

Background radiation comes from the Sun.

Radiation from the Earth

Some rocks contain radioactive materials that affect the soil and water around them. Granite and other volcanic rocks are most likely to contain radioactive material. Although most background radiation is harmless, these rocks can sometimes release the gas radon, which is dangerous to life.

Many homes have smoke detectors. These contain radioactive material.

Manufactured radiation

Some everyday radiation comes from the use of manufactured radioactive materials. If you have an X-ray, you are exposed to radiation. Smoke detectors use a tiny amount of a radioactive substance. None of this radiation is very harmful. The effects of the nuclear industry have also released radiation into our atmosphere. Nuclear explosions and leaks from nuclear power stations have contributed about 0.6 percent of the background radiation found in the atmosphere.

◆ Science in action

Test invisible forces

You will need a bar magnet, a piece of paper, and iron filings. (Ask your science teacher for these.)

Sprinkle the iron filings on the piece of paper. Hold the paper over a bar magnet and see what happens to the iron filings. You have just detected a magnetic force that is invisible to the eye, just as radiation is.

Geiger counters measure radioactivity.

Measuring radioactivity

Scientist Hans Geiger invented a device to measure radioactivity. The Geiger counter clicks when it gets near radioactive material. The more the counter clicks, the higher the level of radiation.

Nuclear power stations

During the last 50 years, scientists have developed ways of using the energy released from the atom to create an energy industry. Nuclear power stations today supply about 20 percent of the world's electrical energy. Some countries such as France use nuclear power to generate about 75 percent of the electrical energy they need.

Nuclear reactors

A *nuclear reactor* creates electrical energy for use in homes and workplaces. The reactor uses the energy released when an atom's nucleus is split. This process is called *nuclear fission*.

This power plant in Brokdorf, Germany, runs on nuclear power.

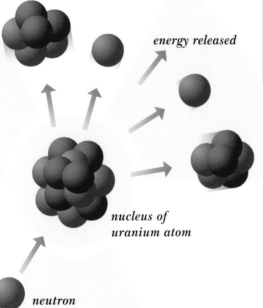

energy released

nucleus of
uranium atom

neutron

Nuclear fission

The atoms of radioactive elements can be split into two smaller pieces. The element with the easiest nucleus to split is uranium. The large uranium atom is unstable and releases neutrons. These neutrons bump into other uranium atoms and cause them to split, resulting in a *chain reaction*. A huge amount of energy is released from such a chain reaction. Nuclear power stations are built so this energy can be released safely. If the reaction is uncontrolled, a nuclear explosion results.

Power stations

The uranium used in a nuclear power station is contained in fuel rods. These are surrounded by *control rods*, *coolant fluid*, and a concrete shield. The control rods make sure that the chain reaction does not happen too fast. Nuclear fission produces energy in the form of heat. The coolant fluid takes this heat away from the reactor core and uses it to heat water to create steam. The steam powers a *generator* that produces electricity.

Built for safety

For safety, the rods and fluid are contained in a steel vessel especially designed to withstand very high temperatures. The whole reactor is enclosed in a concrete building to stop the gamma rays from escaping.

When the fuel rods have to be changed, the workers use machines to handle them.

◆ Science in action

You will need a test tube, sand, thermometer, and stopwatch.

Put some sand in the test tube and take its temperature. With your thumb over the end, time yourself in shaking the test tube for two minutes. Again take the sand's temperature. Has it changed? Why?

This experiment shows how movement energy (shaking) becomes heat energy. In the same way, movement energy of a nuclear chain reaction becomes heat energy.

Working in a nuclear power station

All workers are checked for radioactivity.

People who work in a nuclear power station must be sure they are never exposed to radioactive material. They wear protective clothing and handle radioactive material from a distance with mechanical arms behind glass partitions. The workers are regularly checked for radioactivity to make sure they have not been affected.

Nuclear safety fears

Just as generators using fossil fuels create unwanted waste products, so do nuclear power stations. Most of the waste from a nuclear power station is radioactive.

Nuclear waste has to be stored for many years in special barrels.

This sign warns that something radioactive is behind this fence.

Never safe

Uranium, plutonium, and other fuels used by nuclear power stations continue to release radiation even after they have been used—sometimes for billions of years. Some of these fuels will never be completely safe.

Radiation sickness

A large dose of radiation kills a large number of body cells. The effect is similar to being badly burned. Radiation also affects cell division, the process by which tissues reproduce themselves or grow. The damage can lead to cancer.

These children's illnesses were caused by radiation from a nuclear plant explosion.

Radioactive pollution affects streams.

Public concerns

People living near a nuclear power station are often concerned that their environment might be affected by radiation leaks into the water system or into the land. They fear the possibility of a nuclear meltdown, where the reactor explodes, releasing radiation into the atmosphere. All power stations create waste, so people are concerned that the waste is dealt with safely. The nuclear industry is aware of these fears. The industry campaigns to tell people how carefully it monitors the environment around its sites. The industry spends millions of dollars on research to develop more effective ways of dealing with waste.

Decommissioning

The most significant waste in the nuclear industry is the power station itself. When a power station ends its useful life, it needs to be shut down. The process of shutting down a nuclear power station is called decommissioning. The reactor building is the most awkward to shut down because it still contains radioactive material. The industry's only solution is to cover the whole building with thick layers of concrete to contain the radioactivity.

◆ Sustainable solution

The wind, flowing water, the Sun, the sea, and hot springs called geysers are natural sources of energy. These sources help generate electricity. The wind turns enormous turbines, dams use the force of rushing water, solar panels (right) pick up energy from the Sun, and wave-power systems use the sea's waves to make electricity. These sources of energy are neverending and nonpolluting. They are called renewable energy sources.

Dealing with waste

The objects and equipment used in nuclear power stations can be affected by radioactivity. Even the workers' clothing is treated as nuclear waste. It is considered contaminated, or made dangerous, by radiation.

National waste policies

There are no international agreements on how to deal with any form of nuclear waste. Some countries do not even have a national policy for dealing with waste. Ocean dumping, burial, and reprocessing are some methods used.

Very low-level waste may be dumped in ordinary landfill sites.

Low-level waste

Waste with little radioactivity is called low-level waste. This includes waste rock from uranium mines, the clothing of scientists working with radioactive materials, and material used in hospitals for X-rays. Usually, low-level waste is dumped with nonradioactive waste in sites that are then covered with a layer of soil. This covering is enough of a barrier to the radiation.

Ocean dumping

Some low-level waste is sealed in steel drums and dumped in the ocean. Great Britain's main form of waste disposal was dumping into the Atlantic Ocean. In 1983, the government ended this policy of dumping.

Barrels of nuclear waste are sometimes dumped in the sea.

Concrete is used to prevent radioactive leaks.

Intermediate waste

The next level of waste, called intermediate, cannot be dealt with so simply. This material is much more radioactive than low-level waste and needs to be disposed of more carefully. Usually, intermediate waste is encased in steel and concrete and stored near the power station that created it.

Steel drums of nuclear waste have been covered in concrete before being buried.

Burial

The latest planning on how to deal with intermediate waste is to bury it. The site has to be carefully constructed to ensure complete safety for many years, because intermediate waste remains radioactive for hundreds of years. The steel drums containing the waste are covered in concrete and then buried in a pit lined with more concrete. Above the pit, another layer of concrete is constructed as a further safety precaution.

High-level waste

The fuel rods in a reactor sometimes need replacing as the radioactive material completes its half-life. These fuel rods are high-level waste. Taking apart nuclear weapons also produces high-level waste. The most dangerous parts of the waste need to be safely stored. The main concern about this waste is that it will remain harmful for more than 100,000 years.

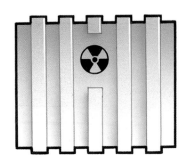

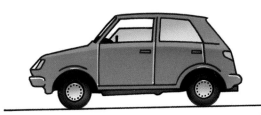

Amount of high-level waste

Power stations produce only a small amount of high-level waste every year. The amount is about the size of a small car. But even this small amount can do great damage and must be stored safely.

Water pools

Neutron radiation does not pass through water, so some power stations keep their high-level waste not just in steel and concrete, but also in water pools. These pools were created as a temporary storage place until the material could be dealt with elsewhere. However, some waste has been in water pools for 20 years. These pools are running out of space.

Used fuel rods from nuclear power stations are very high-level waste.

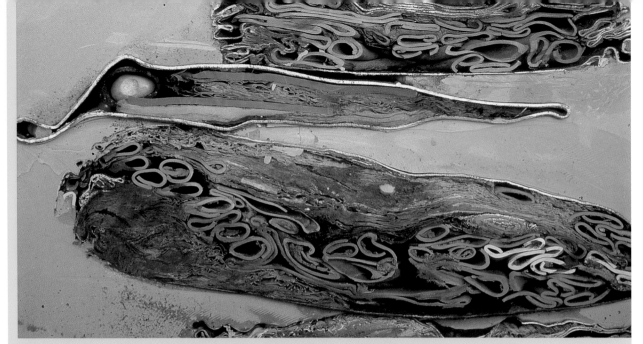
This nuclear waste has been covered in glass and cement for storage.

Burial

The nuclear industry plans to encase high-level waste in glass, which does not decay, and then bury it in deep mines. The mines must be kept open. If scientists discover a way to make the waste safe, it can be brought back to the surface and treated.

Yucca Mountain mine.

◆ Science in action

You will need 2 apples, 2 pieces of paper, 2 plastic bags, and soil.

Take one apple, one piece of paper, and one plastic bag and place them on the window sill. Bury the other set in some soil. After a week, record what happened to each item, both in and out of the soil.

Different objects decay at different rates of time. Some objects such as the plastic bag never decay unless treated in some way. All waste needs to be disposed of carefully to avoid creating garbage that never disappears.

Concerns with burial

Because the waste remains dangerous for so long, the areas chosen for burial must be extremely stable. There should be no threat of earthquakes. The level of water in the ground should not rise to meet the waste, and few people should live in the area. Such sites are not easy to find. In the United States, scientists picked a site in Yucca Mountain, Nevada, for deep mine burial. But scientists believe earthquakes could occur in this area. The mountain range once was volcanic, and scientists are trying to predict whether a volcanic eruption will occur in the next 100,000 years.

Further research

No safe way exists to dispose of high-level nuclear waste. The nuclear power industry raises billions of dollars to research answers to long-term disposal.

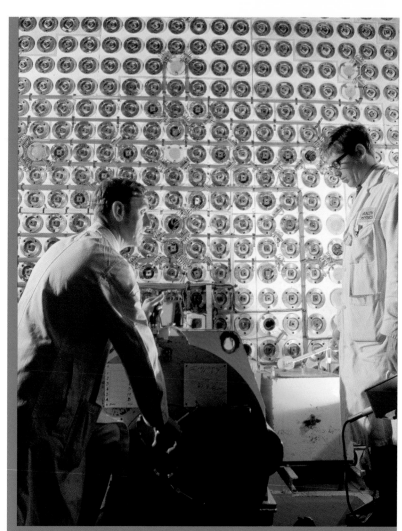

These scientists work in the nuclear laboratories at Harwell in the United Kingdom.

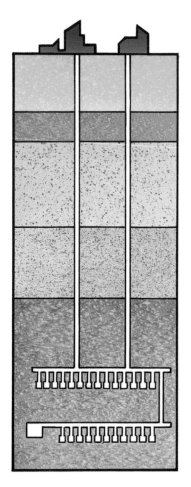

One possible disposal solution is to dispose of nuclear waste in deep underground holes.

Other disposal methods

In the short term, nuclear scientists have worked on safer methods of disposal. Scientists have suggested pouring radioactive material into deep holes in the ground. The material should be so hot that it melts the rock. The rock and material then mix and cool. It is not clear how much radioactivity would escape during such a process. Scientists have also suggested placing waste in holes drilled in the ocean floor. However, if radiation leaked, it could seriously damage the nearby sea life.

Efficient use of nuclear fuel

Some nuclear reactors can create more fuel than they use. These breeder reactors have been developed to make fuel last 50 times longer than fuel in standard nuclear processors.

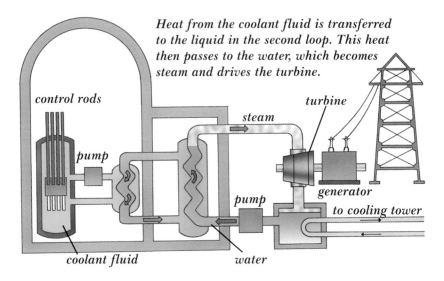

Heat from the coolant fluid is transferred to the liquid in the second loop. This heat then passes to the water, which becomes steam and drives the turbine.

control rods

turbine

steam

pump

generator

to cooling tower

pump

coolant fluid

water

Scientific solutions

The nuclear industry pays scientists to study converting radioactive material to a stable substance. Research focuses on speeding up the process of atomic change and the release of radiation, so the radioactive material becomes harmless. Another possibility involves using a different form of nuclear reaction called *nuclear fusion*.

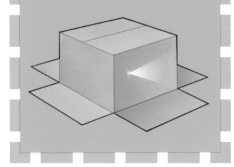

Used fuel rods are reprocessed at this plant in Sellafield, Cumbria, United Kingdom.

Reprocessing

Nuclear scientists have developed ways to change spent fuel rods back into usable fuel. Scientists believe instead of having to find storage places for used fuel rods, the industry can use the same fuel and not have to store it. As a result, less uranium is dug from the ground, and there is less waste to store.

Nuclear fusion

Nuclear reactors work by nuclear fission. Atoms are split to release energy. Another way atoms change, called nuclear fusion, occurs when atoms combine. Fusion releases huge amounts of energy.

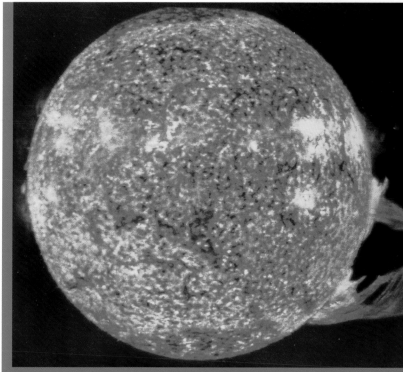

Nuclear fusion happens continuously inside the Sun and in other stars of the universe.

two different types of hydrogen nuclei fuse together

helium nucleus

energy released

electron

The Sun and stars

Nuclear fusion occurs continuously in the Sun and stars. Fusion is the most common form of nuclear reaction in the universe. Nuclear fusion results when hydrogen, the main element on a star, fuses with another hydrogen atom to become helium. The pressure of gravity causes the fusion and results in the release of enormous amounts of heat. When a star's temperature becomes higher than 50 million°F (28 million°C), a reaction occurs.

Recreating fusion

Scientists work to recreate nuclear fusion in the laboratory. Nuclear fusion uses hydrogen, which is readily available. If nuclear fusion could be recreated, less mining of fossil fuels and less work with radioactive materials would be needed.

Pollution-free energy

Another major benefit of nuclear fusion is it does not create radioactive waste. Unlike fission, fusion does not run out of control and cause a massive explosion.

Seas and lakes are sources of the hydrogen needed for nuclear fusion.

The problems

Recreating nuclear fusion requires high pressure and temperature. Scientists may be able to use lasers to help recreate the conditions found in the stars. Scientists hope to achieve nuclear fusion soon. This achievement would mean that the reactors of today are just stepping stones in the direction of unlimited fuel and pollution-free energy.

Lasers help scientists study the stars. In the future, lasers may be used to recreate the conditions needed for nuclear fusion.

Public concerns

Environmental organizations such as Greenpeace work to make the public aware of the dangers of nuclear power and its waste. As a result, people are concerned about living near power stations, near waste disposal sites, and along the routes where nuclear waste is transported.

Environmental organizations such as Greenpeace work for public safety.

The container being unloaded from this ship in France contains used nuclear fuel.

Transportation

In the United States, Europe, and other countries, nuclear fuel and nuclear waste are transported from power stations to storage sites. This transportation has generated public anger, particularly following accidental radiation leaks.

Nuclear protests

In Germany, the government planned to develop a waste storage site in Gorleben, Lower Saxony. People strongly objected, and protesters wrecked the railway lines. In March 1997, 30,000 police were needed to protect the first shipment of nuclear waste from the state of Bavaria to Gorleben.

Site disputes

In 1994, the state of Minnesota allowed Northern States Power (NSP) to store containers of used fuel at its Prairie Island power plant. Storage was allowed on the condition that NSP found a permanent alternative site. Locations identified so far have been turned down by pressure groups. The Mdewakanton Sioux Indians who live on Prairie Island want the fuel removed. Although NSP has nearly filled the storage area, this situation has not been resolved.

The simulator room at Prairie Island nuclear power station.

Public pressure

People can pressure governments to act responsibly regarding nuclear energy policies. For example, in the United States, no nuclear power stations have been built since 1978. In Germany, the new government of 1998 reversed its country's nuclear policy and is committed to closing its 19 nuclear power stations over the next 10 to 20 years.

In 1999, activists demonstrated against the arrival of a truckload of nuclear waste at Rocky Flats Environmental Technology Site in Golden, Colorado.

The future of nuclear powe

The energy industries need to create enough energy to meet people's demands, at the same time producing that energy with acceptable amounts of waste.

Scientists predict that the demand for energy in Asian countries will greatly increase in the next 20 years.

Fossil fuels versus nuclear power

Most scientists agree that the waste gases from fossil fuels create acid rain and smog and contribute to global warming. In 1997, representatives from many countries traveled to Kyoto, Japan, to address these concerns and to reach an agreement on how much fuel they should be using. The agreement is called the Kyoto Protocol. It asks countries to greatly reduce gases contributing to the greenhouse effect. Not every country agreed to the protocol, most notably the United States. Nuclear power does not contribute to greenhouse gases, so some countries see it as a good environmental alternative to using fossil fuels.

Conference participants in Kyoto, Japan, discuss nuclear safety.

Constant source of fuel

Because the nuclear industry does not need huge quantities of fuel, unlike the fossil fuel industry, there is no fear that the minerals used will run out. With new technologies of reprocessing and breeder reactors, the fuel can last even longer.

The fuel inside these rods can be used again if it is reprocessed.

Until scientists find ways to make nuclear waste safe, barrels of nuclear waste will be stored underground.

Research on safety

The nuclear industry is working as quickly as possible to find solutions to waste problems. Nuclear scientists receive funding to solve these problems. Scientists also try to discover how to reproduce pollution-free nuclear fusion. Scientists hope to achieve these goals within the next 50 years.

Further information

These are websites you can use to learn more about topics mentioned in this book.

The British Nuclear Fuel site, located at **www.bnfl.com,** incorporates a section called the Learning Zone especially for children with information and games.

For children's information on nuclear energy with animated cartoons, visit the website at **www.nei.org/scienceclub/index.html**

At the website **www.cleanerandgreener.org,** find ideas and help on living a more energy-efficient life.

Play games and learn about electrical energy at the website located at **www.edisonkids.com**

Gain awareness of energy and its uses by visiting the website located at **www.academyofenergy.org**

The U.S. Department of Energy's Kids Zone, located at **www.energy.gov/kidz/kidzone.html,** offers a variety of activities related to energy.

The site located at **www.globalwarming.com** is sponsored by an environmental protection group dedicated to saving the Earth's natural resources and ending environmental pollution.

The website located at **www.greenpeace.org** explains Greenpeace's views on today's nuclear issues.

Glossary

Atom
The smallest part of a substance that can take part in a chemical reaction.

Carbon dioxide
One of the gases given off when fossil fuels are burned.

Cell
The smallest part of a living being that can exist on its own. Human bodies are made up of millions of cells.

Chain reaction
A rapid series of events in which each event causes the next one. In a nuclear reactor, the chain reaction is the continuous splitting of atoms.

Control rods
Rods that speed up or slow down the chain reaction in a nuclear reactor.

Coolant fluid
A liquid that carries heat from a nuclear reactor to a steam generator.

Emit
To send out or release.

Energy
The power to do work.

Environment
The natural surroundings of an animal or plant.

Forecast
To predict what might happen in the future.

Fossil fuels
Coal, oil, or gas used to produce energy.

Generate
To produce something.

Generator
A machine that changes mechanical energy into electrical energy.

Global warming
The heating of the Earth's atmosphere caused by the greenhouse effect.

Greenhouse effect
The way certain gases in the Earth's atmosphere trap heat rather than allowing it to escape.

Nuclear fission
The splitting of an atom's nucleus to release large amounts of energy.

Nuclear fusion
A reaction caused by combining two atoms to form one heavier nucleus and produce a huge amount of energy. Nuclear fusion happens continuously in the Sun.

Nuclear reactor
A device that generates electrical energy by splitting atoms.

Nucleus
The core of an atom.

Particle
A tiny speck of matter.

Radiation
The invisible rays of energy released by atoms during nuclear fission.

Radioactive
Made of atoms whose cores break down, giving off harmful radiation.

Uranium
The metal used in nuclear reactors.

Index